Families

Grandparents

Revised Edition

Rebecca Rissman

Heinemann Library
Chicago, Illinois

www.capstonepub.com
Visit our website to find out more information about Heinemann-Raintree books.

To order:
☎ Phone 800-747-4992
🖥 Visit www.capstonepub.com
   to browse our catalog and order online.

© 2011, 2021 Heinemann Library
an imprint of Capstone Global Library, LLC
Chicago, Illinois

Edited by Rebecca Rissman and Catherine Veitch
Designed by Ryan Frieson
Picture research by Tracy Cummins
Originated by Capstone Global Library Ltd

Library of Congress Cataloging-in-Publication Data is available on the Library of Congress website.
ISBN 9781484668320 (pb)

Acknowledgments
We would like to thank the following for permission to reproduce photographs: Getty Images: aldomurillo, cover, Alex Mares-Manton, 18, Ariel Skelley, 21, Don Mason, 12, 23, Image Source, 17, Jupiterimages, 9, Kevin Dodge, 14, Kristy-Anne Glubish, 20, Nils Hendrik Muller, back cover, 19, Ron Levine, 16; iStockphoto: Ann Marie Kurtz, 5, Diane Labombarbe, 22; Shutterstock: bbernard, 7, bearinmind, 4, 23, Mehmet Dilsiz, 6, Monkey Business Images, 10, 11, 13, 23, NDAB Creativity, 8, Yarek Gora, 15

We would like to thank Anne Pezalla and Nancy Harris for their invaluable help in the preparation of this book.

Contents

What Is a Family?

A family is a group of people who care for each other.

People in a family are different ages.

All families are different.

All families are special.

What Are Families Like?

Some families like to play games.

Some families like to cook together.

Who Are Grandparents?

Some families have parents. Parents are adults who have children.

grandparent

Parents have parents, too!

They are called grandparents.

Different Grandparents

Your parent's mother is
your grandmother.

Your parent's father is
your grandfather.

Some families have
many grandparents.

Some families have few grandparents.
Some families do not have any
grandparents.

Some grandparents live far from their families.

Some grandparents live with
their families.

Some grandparents care for
their grandchildren.

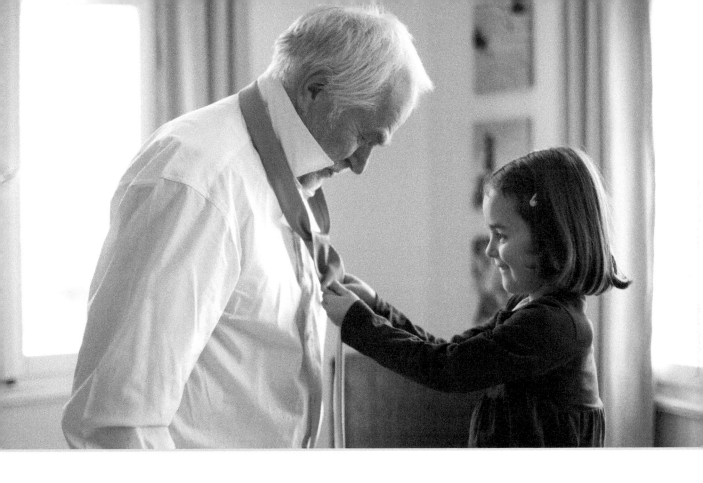

Some grandchildren help care for their grandparents.

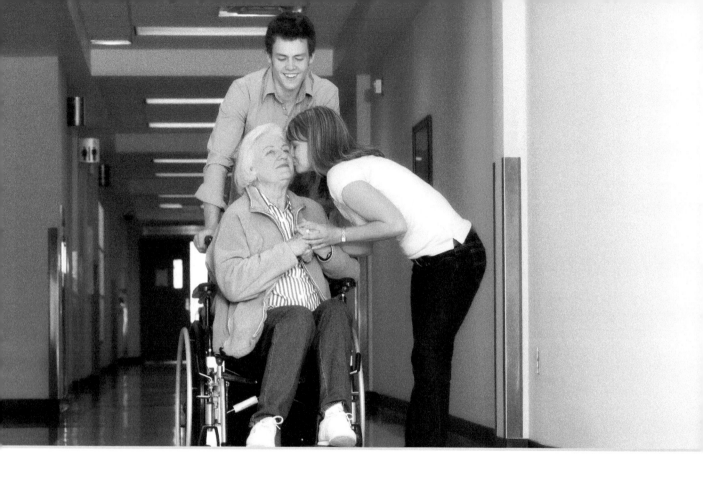

Some families visit their grandparents at special homes.

Do you have grandparents?

Family Tree

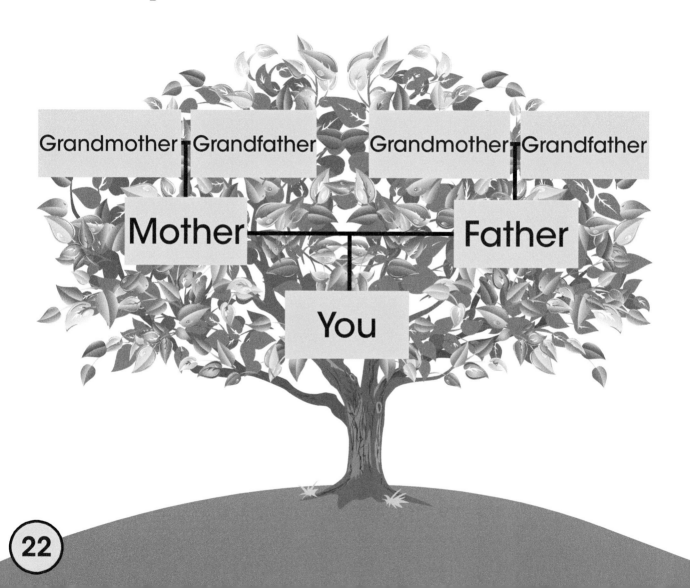

Picture Glossary

grandfather your parent's father

grandmother your parent's mother

parent adult who has children

Index

Note to Parents and Teachers
Before Reading
Explain to children that people in families are often related to each other. Most children are related to their parents. And parents have parents, too! They are a child's grandparents!

After Reading
Ask children if they have special nicknames for their grandparents, such as Grammy or Papa. Make a list of these names on the board.